ROCK CLIMBING

in AUSTRALIA

NEW HOLLAND

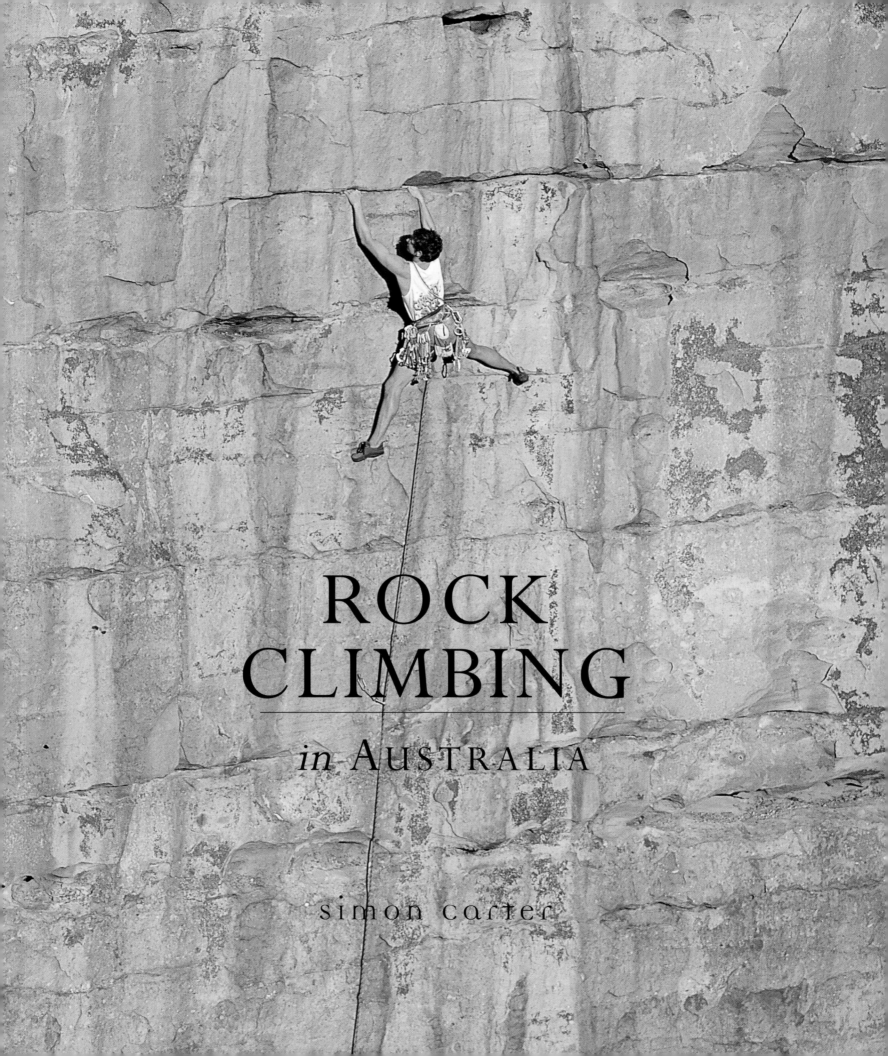

ROCK CLIMBING

in AUSTRALIA

simon carter

First published in Australia in 1998 by New Holland Publishers (Australia) Pty Ltd
Sydney • Auckland • London • Cape Town

Produced and published in Australia by New Holland Publishers (Australia) Pty Ltd
14 Aquatic Drive Frenchs Forest NSW 2086 Australia
1A/218 Lake Road Northcote Auckland New Zealand
24 Nutford Place London W1H 6DQ United Kingdom
80 McKenzie Street Cape Town 8001 South Africa

National Library of Australia Cataloguing-in-Publication Data:

Carter, Simon.
Rock climbing in Australia.
ISBN 1 86436 340 1.
1. Rock climbing - Australia - Pictorial works. I. Title.
796.52230994

Half-title page Enga Lokey, The Edge of
Pleasure (21), Mount Buffalo, Victoria; **Title
page** Greg James, FAB (23), Point Perpendicular,
New South Wales; **Above sequence** Rob
LeBreton, Some Kind of Bliss (32), Diamond
Falls, Blue Mountains, New South Wales.

Publishing General Manager: Jane Hazell
Publisher: Averill Chase
Editor: Anna Sanders
Designer: Trinity Loubser-Fry
Design Assistant: Laurence Lemmon-Warde
Reproduction: Hirt & Carter Cape (Pty) Ltd
Printer: Tien Wah Press (Pte) Ltd

The authors and publishers have made every
effort to ensure the information in this book was
correct at the time of going to press and accept
no responsibility for any inconvenience, loss or
injury sustained by any person using this book.

CONTENTS

DARWIN

NORTHERN TERRITORY

WESTERN
AUSTRALIA

Kalbarri

PERTH

Margaret River

*West
Cape Howe*

Albany

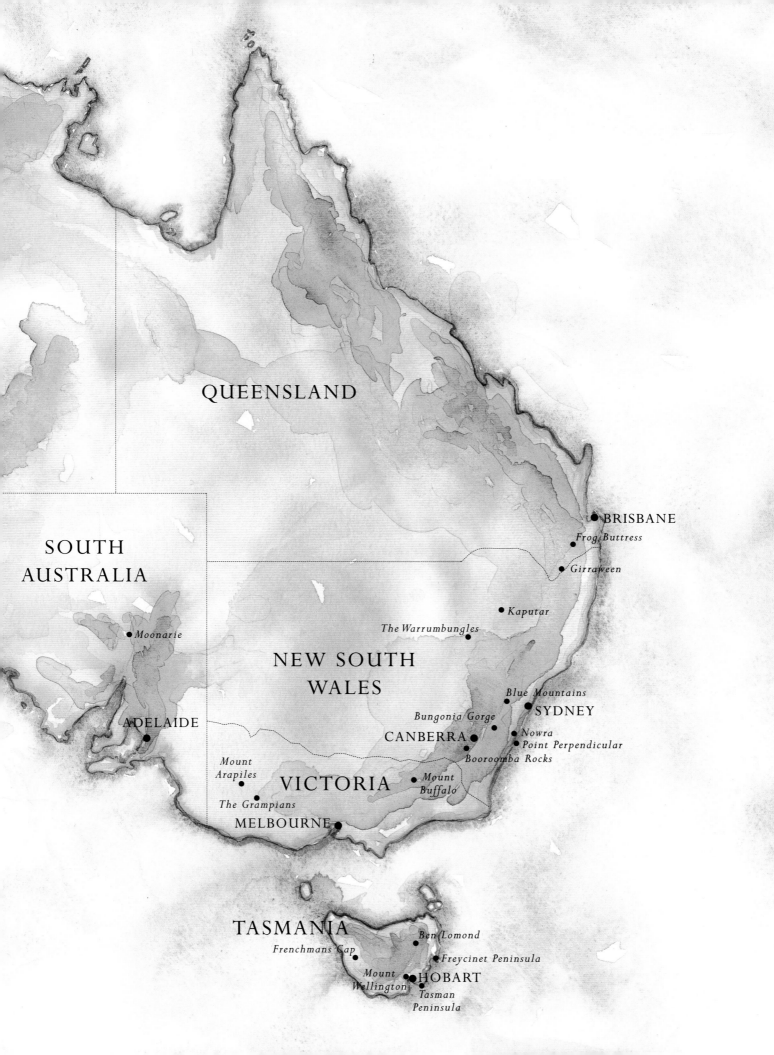

QUEENSLAND

SOUTH
AUSTRALIA

NEW SOUTH
WALES

VICTORIA

TASMANIA

BRISBANE
Frog Buttress

Girraween

Kaputar

The Warrumbungles

Moonarie

Blue Mountains

Bungonia Gorge

SYDNEY

CANBERRA

Nowra
Point Perpendicular

Booroomba Rocks

ADELAIDE

Mount
Arapiles

Mount
Buffalo

The Grampians

MELBOURNE

Ben Lomond

Frenchmans Cap

Freycinet Peninsula

Mount
Wellington

HOBART

Tasman
Peninsula

fOREWORD

When Simon Carter takes a photograph, he darts around the crag like a mild-mannered sub-atomic particle. He is like a photon of concentrated energy, with deeply introspective eyes, and somehow remaining polite to anyone dumb enough to ask him a question while he is in mid-flight.

He has managed to maintain this energy level for four years purposefully documenting the major crags of the entire

Australian continent, with a placid but almost missionary zeal. Just visiting all these places is a major achievement in itself. He could only have kept going by being totally immersed in the scene; by getting a blast out of being on those beautiful wild crags; and by patiently moulding each shot. Now he has crafted his photon sculpture into *Rock Climbing in Australia* by gathering the most talented climbing word-smiths around to interpret their vision of what rock climbing is in Australia.

Simon's images have created some white fella dreaming — stories of rock worshippers on the gnarly teeth which grow from the stunted gums of an old land; ever so soft and vulnerable flesh against hard rock; little climbing specks lost in blue air space which will be as enticing to non-climbers as they are to climbers; climbers drawn in by the primal urge to dance around on steep, warm rock — heads cleansed of other, unnecessary stuff.

These are images that for ever and a day will be distinctly 'Carter photos', his mind's eye, his genre. Clean, hauntingly beautiful shots that you will keep coming back to. Photos that you need to stare into for a while, often with disbelief.

Greg Mortimer

Above *Greg Mortimer at West Cape Howe, Western Australia.*
Opposite *Roxanne Wells, pitch two The Free Route (25), The Totem Pole, Cape Hauy, Tasmania.*

PREFACE

At first glance rock climbing may seem a bizarre concept. Easily dismissed as contrived, reckless, or crazy. Yet rock climbing has always seemed to me such a natural thing to do. It gives you a perfect challenge — mental as well as physical.

Climbing became an essential part of my life soon after I first tried it 15 years ago. Since then, it has also given me good friends, a love of the bush, inspiration for my photography, and the will to follow my dreams.

The combination of rock climbing and photography has become something of an obsession for me. It's a process that began in the early 1990s when, for a few months at a time, I spent over a year camped at Mount Arapiles, dedicated to the climbing lifestyle and climbing as hard as I could. Many climbers around me were doing interesting and newsworthy things, and so on rest days I started to pick up my camera. Perhaps not the most restful of rest day activities but I soon realised I had the perfect subject matter for photography.

Living in the dirt I realised why I loved rock climbing so much. Because it is so different from everyday life. The contrast it gives with our urban world and workday stress could easily be its greatest value. A true recreation, not commercial exploitation, which reconnects us with the natural world in a way that is all too rare. And like the 'travellers eyes' you get after a long trip abroad, we look back on the confusing roar of our information overloaded, stressed-out material world and maybe, just maybe, begin to see life's problems and priorities in new light.

None of this comes without a cost, and as I've learned — far, far too well over the years — rock climbing is dangerous. Personally, I've justified the risk as the price one pays for attempting to live a life less ordinary. It's also a decision not to let fear or needlessly clinging to a comfort zone inhibit me from experiencing some of life's more fascinating possibilities. And it's an acceptance that in climbing, as in life, you may do everything right and still end up maimed. But this is my rationale, a personal decision — it has to be that way.

As recreational climbers we make all our own decisions, from the partner we choose, the climbs we try, the gear we use, the protection and rock we trust, the helmet we (don't) wear, to whether we climb at all, and we live (or otherwise) with the consequences. It is only climbers, individually, who can make these decisions. It's the principle of personal responsibility. Most climbers aren't reckless or crazy.

The combining of both rock climbing and photography has demanded far more effort than I ever imagined — and given me more gripping moments than my climbing alone ever did. Yet, images of climbing on the Totem Pole and Taipan Wall are like frozen moments of perfection for me. They answer the question of 'why climb' far better than my words ever could.

My obsession has turned into something of a photographic and climbing odyssey that has taken me all over our vast land to some of our best, most popular and significant climbing areas. To some of our most beautiful and spectacular places. This book is the result.

Simon Carter

Above *Simon Carter,* Evil D *(29), The Gallery, The Grampians, Victoria.*
Opposite *Stefan Eberhard,* Magic and Loss *(M4, 195 metres), Mount Buffalo, Victoria.*

INTRODUCTION

With so many different experiences to offer, climbing in Australia is truly diverse and splendid. The art of climbing, as portrayed in this book, is a modern one, and very different to that of the sport's early days. Hawser-laid hemp ropes and slings, steel karabiners and hammering in pitons all belong mostly to the past. Modern climbing is a high-tech endeavour with complicated tools of the highest alloys. This technology allows its devotees an activity that is somewhere between chess, dance and athletics — a complex sport that at its highest level requires extreme physical prowess and concentration but that can be enjoyed at other levels by all.

Despite many factions maintaining their claim to be the true chosen ones, the modern face of climbing is not one of bland homogeneity. Climbing now has a huge variety of forms — the difference being mainly in the way the rope is used — that is, bouldering, gym climbing, trad(itional) climbing, adventure climbing, mountaineering, sport climbing and a mixture of these various schools.

At one end of the technology spectrum is aid climbing where the climber pulls on the rope and other devices to get up the climb. This technique was used in the past, particularly in the 1960s and 1970s, to climb some of the steepest and smoothest faces in the world.

Eventually, however, it was predominantly replaced by free climbing, in which the climbers use their hands and feet to climb the rock. Ultimately, the aim of free climbing a route is to make it from the bottom to the top without having to hang on the rope at any time. The rope is there, and clipped to protection points along the way, but it's only to catch you if you fall, not to help you up the rock.

Free climbing should not be confused with free soloing where the climber risks injury or death by climbing high problems unroped. Many climbers never solo and it is very rarely practised anywhere near a climber's technical limit. Also without the hindrance of gear, but safer, is bouldering. This is where the climber, usually with just boots and chalk bag, does short, hard problems, often going sideways just above the ground, on boulders or short walls. Although traditionally used for training, it is often now practised for its own pleasures.

In the early decades of this century, the legendary Dr Eric Dark and other Blue Mountaineers visited areas like Bungonia Gorge and did the first climbs in the volcanic-plug infested Warrumbungles in northern New South Wales. The idea of conquering a summit, betraying rock climbing's origins in mountaineering, was evident in these early ascents. The climbs of these and other pioneers were a long way from modern, short, super-hard routes, yet many aspects of the climbing experience remain the same. It can still be dangerous and exciting. And it still brings to its practitioners the marvellous gift of being outside in Australia's fine bushlands.

In the 1960s Victorian climbers discovered Mount Arapiles and did the first new routes at what was to be for many years Australia's foremost climbing area. In New South Wales, climbers like Bryden Allen, John Ewbank and others in the Sydney Rockclimbing Club were active. The very gifted Ewbank was most influential, pushing the direction of climbing towards shorter gymnastic-style climbs and inventing the grading system that bears his name and is still in use today in Australia, South Africa and New Zealand.

Young Australian climbers increased the difficulty of climbs in the early 1970s. However, the 1974 visit of American 'Hot' Henry Barber most profoundly affected Australian climbing. When he left, Australian climbing had reached the grade of 23 and a whole new generation of climbers were keen to

establish world-class routes. One climber however took to the task with an almost ascetic fanaticism.

Starting out as a talented schoolboy, Sydney climber Kim Carrigan moved to Arapiles and, with training, dieting and a lot of climbing, began to push Australian climbing up to world standards. He established Australia's first 26 with the first free ascent of *Procul Harum* in 1978. In the following years he added the first 27, 28, 29 (*India*), 30 (*Masada*) and only barely failed to put up the first 31, *Lord of the Rings*, which was eventually done by another overseas visitor, German Stefan Glowacz. The importance of Carrigan's

Above left John Ewbank, Defecation *(15), Sublime Point, Blue Mountains, New South Wales, in 1964, aged 16.*

Above right Bryden Allen, Toyland *(25), Cosmic County, Blue Mountains, New South Wales. Climbing harder than ever in 1998 at 58.*

achievements in breaking physical and, more importantly, psychological barriers should not be underestimated.

In the 1980s to climb well it was almost compulsory to live at Arapiles and to climb as much as possible. At the time Arapiles was one of the most relaxed climbing environments in the world. There were climbers from the United States, Japan, New Zealand, England and places far more exotic, all climbing together and sharing the hot dirt of the campsite.

On the climbing front it was visiting German superstar, the late, great Wolfgang Gullich, who finally eclipsed Carrigan's very bright star. In 1985, while attending an International Climbing Meeting at Arapiles, Wolfgang jumped on a project of Swiss visitor Martin Scheel and, after several days' work, managed to climb *Punks in the Gym* (32), a sustained 40-metre overhanging wall on which the number of holds is akin to the population of Antarctica. Years later a crumbling crux hold was 'rebuilt' with glue, and some people feel the climb is now slightly easier than it was. Nevertheless, *Punks* is still very difficult and much coveted. When it was done it was the hardest climb in the world and remained Australia's hardest climb until 1994, when its first Australian ascensionist, Stuart Wyithe, added a reputedly harder variant called *Pretty in Punk*.

Several other developments in the early 1990s were also important for their effect on the sport. Living in the dirt at Arapiles with little recourse to showers and other creature comforts was not for everybody. The advent of climbing gyms and basement training boards made it possible to live in a city, train ferociously, perhaps hold down a job, and still climb harder than ever. This non-nature aspect of climbing, coupled with the introduction of power bolt drills, saw some newer Blue Mountains and Nowra cliffs becoming increasingly fashionable.

The state-of-the-art since the days of Dr Dark has changed faster than a government ministry. Instead of long runouts on easy Warrumbungles' walls, the hardest routes in the country are on short bolt-protected walls, preferably close to a bakery or coffee shop. The most difficult climb in the country may still be 32 but there are many people who can climb close to this grade and who casually cruise climbs that a mere 20 years ago were thought impossible.

There are more climbing areas to choose from now as well. The recumbent quartzite lump of Arapiles is popular with the masses, much to the delight of businesses in the local town of Natimuk. The nearby ranges of blue hills and steep sandstone escarpments, the Grampians, has many separate areas of which the sensational overhanging red Taipan Wall is the jewel in the crown. The alpine plateau of Mount Buffalo, north of Melbourne, is Victoria's premier summer climbing area. The gorge here is home to the mighty 250-metre *Ozymandias Direct* which is a popular aid route and, free at 28, it is the country's longest 'hard' route. Also on the plateau are some of Australia's most stylish slab routes.

In New South Wales the Blue Mountains is replete with sandstone, evident in many fine crags and the long, steep walls of the Grose and Wolgan valleys. It is still the main

Above *The Glass House Mountains, south-eastern Queensland, scene of some of Australia's earliest rock climbing.*

climbing area in the state. South of Sydney, the short, steep sandstone walls at Nowra are very popular, especially in winter, and hold a good percentage of Australia's modern hard climbs. Near here climbers hang high above the blue waters of Jervis Bay on the atmospheric Point Perpendicular. Inland, the huge, steep gorge of Bungonia supplies a kind of methadone program for European-limestone addicts, and for those whose tastes run more to granite there is the excellent area of Booroomba, near Canberra. North of Sydney the Warrumbungles is still important as an alpine training ground and, north again, there is the geologically similar but smaller area of Kaputar. East of here, Armidale maintains its small but dedicated climbing population.

In Queensland, the climbing population suffers from extensive access problems, with many of the grand crags off-limits. The superb jam cracks of Frog Buttress remain indispensable and there are also fine climbs on Girraween's granite outcrops and domes. The jutting volcanic plugs of the Glasshouse Mountains, north of Brisbane, were the site of some of Australia's earliest climbing and still sport popular, if at times loose and dangerous, routes. In the far north, Mount Stuart, overlooking Townsville, hints at the state's undiscovered potential.

South Australia's main problem for climbing lies in its being Australia's flattest state. However Morialta Gorge, near Adelaide, is more popular than ever and spending a week in the subtle-hued deserts at Moonarie remains one of Australia's best climbing experiences.

In recent years a few activists have been busy in the Northern Territory around Alice Springs and Darwin. In Western Australia an incredibly keen climbing population pushes standards on the beautiful Kalbarri cliffs, north of Perth. This area has greatly added to the climbing potential in the West and acts as a counterpoint to the great, but occasionally weather-ridden, areas around Albany, and the small but pretty crags around Margaret River.

Tasmanian climbers have not been idle either, developing areas such as Freycinet Peninsula, Adamsfield, Hobart's Mount Wellington and the Tasman Peninsula. This island state still remains the destination for adventure climbers with awesome cliffs like 300-plus metre Frenchmans Cap, Precipitous Bluff and Geryon. If the world's governments continue their myopic greenhouse policies, then in the future the Apple Isle may be the only place in Australia not too hot to climb — although the sea cliffs will be slightly shorter!

In the short-term however, global warming is being overshadowed by other threats to climbing. Some land managers, whether private or government, see climbing as an insignificant part of recreational land use, one that is easier to regulate and ban than incorporate into their area. While some ecological restrictions are understandable, a climate of litigation and fear brought on by the anti-commonsense precedents from the United States is not. Yet climbing is subject to strict controls in New South Wales national parks for this very reason. Unfortunately the more anarchic attitude of many climbers, admittedly part of climbing's strength and attraction, has not helped with the communication necessary with such land managers. Care and commonsense are needed on both sides of the problem.

This book is a record not only of the many faces of modern Australian rock climbing, but also of wild areas in which climbers' liberty is constantly under threat. It is a record of a sport in which passion and effort are rewarded with creations of outstanding beauty. It is a document of a sport in which the human body and mind are dragged far from the urbane world of the horizontal literally to a higher plane.

The Australian climbing scene, though expanding, is still relatively small and friendly. As a nation of crag climbers, as opposed to mountaineers, we appreciate those thousands of little days spent lying around the base of some climb with friends whilst above someone puts themselves through physical and/or mental anguish on the end of the rope.

The effort, the passion, the pain, the coffee afterwards. This is what it is all about.

Greg Pritchard

BLUE MOUNTAINS

No-one knows what makes the Blue Mountains blue. Some say the mysterious steely haze that tints these highlands is the work of sunlight filtering through tiny airborne droplets of eucalyptus oil. But it is only a theory.

What I know for sure about the Blue Mountains is that this urban wilderness of sandstone cliffs, ferny grottoes and watery cascades is, for me, the most climbable landscape on earth. Perhaps I'm biased because it's here that I found climbing. In the early 1970s my teenage pals and I would catch the train up from Sydney after school, get off at Katoomba or Mount Victoria, and then, burdened by ill-fitting rucksacks crammed with ropes, steel carabiners and canned sardines, we'd shamble by torchlight through leg-slicing heath to camping caves.

The deity of Australian climbing then was John Ewbank and we revered his witty, opinionated guidebook, *Rock Climbs in the Blue Mountains*. Schoolboyish were our dreams to repeat his aid routes on that tottering hulk, Dogface, which appeared in 1929 when a huge slice of cliff collapsed. Scrawny-armed were our designs on his hardest climb, *Janicepts*, graded 21 with some rests on protection along the way. On a chilly spring day in 1974, I watched Michael Law, then 15 years old, make the first free ascent of *Janicepts*.

Michael, 'Claw', went on to develop hundreds of routes in the mountains, and write his own guidebook too. I'm still perusing the guide, still dreaming of falling up routes that he, Giles Bradbury, John Smoothy, Mark Baker, and a younger set, have established. As I write, the hardest route in the mountains is 11 grades harder than the *Janicepts* of my youth.

A rock climb is, I suppose, a sequence of moves, a set of holds, a bit of gear to ease the risk, a flurry of human energy and desire — and then it's over. But in the Blue Mountains, a more lasting dimension — the landscape — enters the climber. When I am old, I know I'll recall cragging with friends amid the screech of black cockatoos around Centennial Glen and Porters Pass; lightning bolts, cannonades of thunder and monsoonal downpours emptying from Himalayan-tall thunderheads onto Cosmic County and the Freezer; the roar of winter wind ripping across the Shipley Plateau; the solar blaze of Piddingtons Flank as the sun drops behind the Kanimbla Valley; the bristling of the hair on your sweating arms as you muscle up a sea of sandstone and see a tide of fog welling out of the Grose Valley and rolling over Blackheath.

Scatter my ashes here.

NEW SOUTH WALES
Blue Mountains • • *Sydney*

Greg Child

Previous pages Julian Saunders, Daedalus *(28), Taipan Wall, The Grampians, Victoria.*
Above Waratah.
Opposite Giles Bradbury, pitch three Giant *(24, 110 metres), Dogface.*

Left *Simon Mentz (top) and Steve Monks contemplate pitch four* Titan *(26, 120 metres), Dogface.*

Above *Steve Monks belaying and Adam Darragh, pitch three* Echo Crack *(25, 190 metres), Echo Point, Katoomba.*

Below *Greg Child,* Day of Reckoning *(21), Narrowneck.*

Opposite *Garth Miller, project, Diamond Falls.*

Opposite top and bottom Rob LeBreton, Some Kind of Bliss
(32), Diamond Falls.

Above left Catherine Destivelle, Day of Reckoning *(21), Narrowneck.*

Above right Bobbi Bensman, Rubber Lover *(25), Wave Wall.*

Left Nick Sutter, Oranges Poranges *(24), Hanging Rock.*

Above Richard Rogers and Greg Moore belaying, Black Rose *(27), Hanging Rock.*

Below Dawn in the Grose Valley.

Above left *Garth Miller.*

Above right *John Smoothy.*

Sequence *Garth Miller,* Teenage Nervous
Breakdown *(26), Corroboree Walls.*

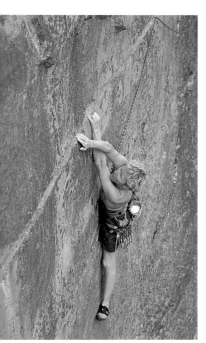

Left *Greg Child pitch two* The Prozac Years *(25), Shipley Lower. Pitches are 24, 25 and 21.*

Above *Greg Moore following and Greg Child belaying, pitch two* The Prozac Years.

Below *Greg Child belaying pitch three* The Prozac Years.

Opposite *Frey Yule and Brendan Junge belaying,* Super Trance 2000 *(23), Pierces Pass.*

Opposite *Silvia Fitzpatrick, pitch three* Bladderhozen *(23), Pierces Pass.*
Pitches are 21, 21, and 23.

Above left *Steve Monks,* Disco Non-stop Party *(25), Pierces Pass.*

Above right *Catherine Destivelle,* Fear in the Western World *(22),*
Cosmic County.

BUNGONIA GORGE

Bungonia Gorge has long fired the imagination, providing routes with epic reputations and a terrifying atmosphere. Cleaved through a limestone slab more than 300 metres thick, the canyon has a history of tension and high drama — a boulevard of long routes, shattered egos and broken dreams.

Climbing in the gorge is unpredictable. On good days it feels like paradise. The descent track weaves through a rainforest sanctuary studded with grass trees and lyrebirds. The gorge appears abruptly, 200 vertical metres of limestone on the north side, over 300 metres on the south, separated by a narrow ribbon of water-polished boulders. The climbing is superb, lunging between perfectly formed pockets, orange rock, mind-blowing threads for runners, and inspiring stalactites either side.

On bad days it can be terrifying. The black walls tower forebodingly and a cold, evil wind howls up the gorge. The holds are slippery and brittle, the sections of loose rock longer, and the pockets riddled with cobwebs.

John Fantini has been king of the gorge for over a decade. The routes he made in the early 1980s in the ground-up style of the day defy comprehension. Routes like *Jewel Box*, *Comet Chaser* and *Reason for Man* — all long, loose, runout and hard. Much of the reason Bungonia remained 'undiscovered' until more recent times stemmed from John's ability to climb new routes, on sight, on loose rock, with poor protection, at grades harder than anyone was prepared to repeat.

Times began to change with the arrival of Tony Barten, Andrew Bull, a new top-down ethic and a drill. The late 1980s and early 1990s saw the construction of a number of well-protected routes at

Bungonia Gorge. *Siblings of the Sun* and *Albino* climb the height of the south wall with good gear and sound rock all the way. Fantini joined the top-down new wave with enthusiasm, putting his stamp on this gigantic wall with the instant classic *Overture to the Sun*. More recently the top and bottom pitches of the gorge have seen attention from those with the ability to pull down very hard, yielding high-grade, single-pitch, bolted routes.

Climbers have hardly scratched the surface of Bungonia's potential. Only recently Andrew McAuley created the seven-pitch extravaganza *Evolution* simply by throwing his abseil ropes from the gorge's rim and climbing where they lay. It seems that as climbers dream longer and grow stronger Bungonia Gorge is destined to become Australia's premier long crag.

Kieran Lawton

Above *Chris Jones — 'top-down' access to the South Wall.*
Opposite *Chris Jones and Mike Weeks belaying, pitch six (25)* Overture to the Sun *(26).*
Pitches are 21, 21, 23, 24, 23, 25 and 26.

Above *Tony Barten and Andrew Bull belaying, pitch seven (crux), Siblings of the Sun (26). Pitches are 21, 21, 23, 22, 21, 24, 26 and 16.*

Above *Andrew McAuley, pitch six (crux) Evolution (24). Pitches are 17, 22, 21, 23, 22, 24 and 23.*

Left *John Fantini, Jumpmaster (23, M1) first ascent, later freed at 26.*

Opposite *Robyn Cleland and Pat Deavoll belaying pitch seven (crux) Siblings of the Sun (26).*

Following pages *Mike Weeks, pitch seven (crux) Overture to the Sun (26).*

KAPUTAR

How do you characterise climbing at Kaputar? How do you capture the contentment of sitting on a belay ledge part-way up the Governor, basking in the first of the morning sun? The relief of reaching the summit half an hour after sunset? The sheer beauty of the place? Let me try . . .

Although there are three main climbing venues in the Kaputar National Park — Ningadhun, Euglah Rock and the Governor — it's the Governor that is the star attraction. This cliff's dominant feature is a massive set of roofs which overhang an attractive mosaic wall by some 15 metres. These roofs stretch across about 100 metres of the main face, but only a few routes manage to thread their way through them, and only one tackles them head-on — the *Great Barrier Roof*. This route was first climbed in 1979 and has had few ascents since then. Still, it might be argued that this climb epitomises rock climbing at Kaputar.

The *Great Barrier Roof* winds its way through some of the most hostile territory imaginable. Indeed, it looks much harder than the meagre 23 it receives in the guidebook, but the difficulties, as with so many climbs at Kaputar, are psychological rather than physical. For example, you're frequently required to commit to an apparently long, unprotected section only to be pleasantly surprised by a runner placement once you move up.

There's also the exposure, which often belies the 80–90 metres height of the cliff. This is never more striking than after you traverse out to the hanging arete which leads to the *Great Barrier Roof*'s second tier of overhangs. It usually requires a few trips out there before one acclimatises enough to think about anything other than retreating!

As for the rock. In typical Kaputar fashion, it ranges from superb, chocolate-brown trachyte to . . . well, let's just say it varies. When I did the *Great Barrier Roof* several years ago, I inadvertently kicked the lip of a roof as I pulled through the second tier of overhangs. I was horrified to hear what sounded like the whole of the Governor's central roofs resonating like cathedral bells! Yet once above this section, I was treated to some of the best rock Australia has to offer.

I could go on, but I suspect that in the end whatever I say will fail to convey the spirit of climbing at Kaputar. Climbing in this fantastic place really needs to be experienced first-hand.

Mark Colyvan

Above *The Governor.*
Opposite *Peter Wehr, Ay Caramba (22), Euglah Rock.*

Above *Peter Wehr*, Live Bait *(23)*, *The Governor.*

Opposite *Danelle Rae*, Blood on the Moon *(21)*, *The Governor.*

NOWRA

The backyards of suburban Nowra on the New South Wales South Coast are the last place you would expect to find one of Australia's finest climbing areas. So it's surprising to discover that the cliffs along the Shoalhaven River and Bomadery Creek provide an array of high-quality rock climbing that can boast Australia's highest concentration of hard routes and attracts climbers from all over the country.

'History' and 'Nowra' are not two words normally used together by most climbers. Yet Nowra has perhaps been the most important place in recent Australian climbing history. The development of Nowra is basically the evolution of sport climbing in Australia. In the early 1990s local climbers, inspired by what they'd seen happening in Europe and America, went against tradition and established routes where the emphasis was on pushing their physical limits. Routes were set up to maximise the athleticism and enjoyment of climbing, and to minimise the amount of fiddling with gear required. As a result, standards soared and a flow-on effect was felt through the rest of the Australian climbing scene as other climbers adopted sport climbing tactics and attitudes.

The original rivalry that occurred between the new sport climbers and traditional climbers has long since petered out as both parties realised that sport climbing was not here to replace traditional climbing, but rather complement it nicely. The crags at Nowra have gone on to produce more hard climbs and good climbers than any other area in Australia in recent times.

The rock around Nowra is ideally suited to sport climbing. It's very solid, highly featured sandstone with a smooth water-polished finish. More often than not it is very, very steep. You can forget the wilderness experience here — your average Nowra route forces its way out of the back of a dark, dank cave and rarely makes it above the tree line. Many visitors to the area are turned off by the urban environment and the severity of the climbs. There are very few climbers who can come here and immediately climb at their normal standard. The powerful nature of the routes, the complexity of the rock and the ever-present humidity take a lot of getting used to. Yet Nowra locals are one of the most area-loyal and psyched group of climbers in Australia today. Maybe it's because they've had to put in the effort to appreciate this unique rock, and have really earned their ability to climb here.

Rob LeBreton

NEW SOUTH WALES

Sydney

Nowra

Above *Matt Adams taping up; demonstrating a 'stick clip'; and with Chris Jones at South Central.*
Opposite *Andrew Bull,* Conehead and the Barbiturates *(28), The Grotto.*

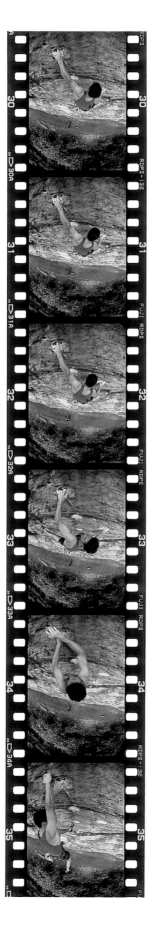

Previous pages: film sequence *Andrew Bull,* Hard Candy *(27), PC. Motordrive at 4.2 frames per second;* **right** *Rod Young,* Cowboy Junkies *(26), Thompson's Point.*

Above *Julian Saunders,* Narcosis *(30), Thompsons Point.*

Right *Matt Adams,* Maintain the Rage *(27), South Central.*

Left *Zac Vertrees*, Stone Roses *(26), Thompsons Point.*

Above *Matt Adams*, Pulling on Porcelain *(23), Thompsons Point.*

Below *Tara Sutherland*, Concrete Petunias *(28), Thompsons Point.*

POINT PERPENDICULAR

The sky is big over Point Perpendicular. Surrounded by blue, the cliffs seem suspended — a vertical cascade of sandstone, in places solid, in places sandy honeycomb; rotten, eaten and gouged, eroded by wind and water. And at the bottom, the sea, the sea, that moody animal: skittish, playful kitten; crashing, vengeful monster. Filling the air with an ever-present sound, filling the lungs with salty seaweed ozone taste.

The first time I was there the wind was so strong it was like a cushion — you could lean out from the cliff and gravity had no pull. Voices were torn away before the sound was out of your mouth. The sea was crashing below, thrown into white-capped chaos. The ropes came back in your face. But many more days have been sunkissed and still, the rock below beckoning invitingly. The climbing game is to play the tease between pushing your limits or playing it safe, getting gripped or cruising, launching into the unknown or repeating a classic.

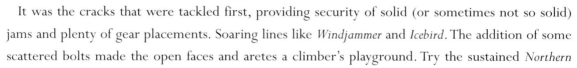

It was the cracks that were tackled first, providing security of solid (or sometimes not so solid) jams and plenty of gear placements. Soaring lines like *Windjammer* and *Icebird*. The addition of some scattered bolts made the open faces and aretes a climber's playground. Try the sustained *Northern Exposure* or feel the airyness of *Liquid Insanity*. A full set of cams, if not two sets, is advisable. The horizontal breaks just seem to eat them up. And double ropes, no dead straight line of bolts and chalked-up holds here. It's committing to abseil over the edge, especially to a hanging belay. Am I in the right place? Will I be able to get out? A set of prusiks can be necessary and very reassuring. And so the climbing takes you, pulling you towards the top, the moves singing, the gear slotting into place. From the pocket to the break, a tiny edge. Am I getting pumped? Was that the crux? Hey, this is good! To the top and the belay, to gaze out across the ocean, to watch for whales, sharks, dolphins or the sea-birds plunging into the waves. And listen for the quack of penguins and the eternal singing sound of the sea.

So get down there, experience it for yourself. Lean over the edge, launch into the unknown, get committed. Snuff the ozone, do the moves, feel the power of the ocean, the prickle of fear, the elation of success. It's all climbing.

Robyn Cleland

Above *Looking north from Windjammer Wall.*
Opposite *Robyn Cleland,* Liquid Insanity *(23), Lighthouse Area.*

Above *Greg James,* FAB *(23), Thunderbird Wall.*

Opposite *Catherine Destivelle,* Rex Hunt's Lovechild *(20),*
Lighthouse Area.

Left *Catherine Destivelle,* Thunderbirds are Bogged *(23),* ThunderbirdWall.

Above *Mike Moore,* Some Weird Sin *(24),WindjammerWall.*

Sydney Sea Cliffs

The Sydney sea cliffs are one of those great concepts that just never sold — in a consumer-based society they are just too serious for fun and too convenient for the adventure required by adrenaline junkies and mountaineers. It seems close to all amenities, but see how easy it is to get rescued climbing on the backside of suburbia. It's more remote than Antarctica.

The presence of a horizon and the flat ocean at the bottom of the cliffs, like Arapiles, enhances verticality. Loose bits falling away have left the cliffs with the perfect architecture for fantasy, the otherworldly arches and roofs are enhanced by the heaving, spiking sea below — when seagulls are below and inland, you know it's steep.

Moods and grades can change in a few minutes. I've seen dolphins and seals in the sun, and nearly been hit by suicidal projectiles. I've cruised flawless sports routes with awesome moves, and had my belayer washed away.

On a sunny day, with deep green water, sun-warmed rock and an easy climb, it's all very sweet. Let the wind pick up a bit, the holds slope the wrong way, get a little bit lost and suddenly you're waist-deep. No matter what grade it is, once you start shouting over the waves at your belayer, blood pressure and gravity both rise sharply. As Greg Child said, 'The crux of a climb is rarely the hardest move'.

The whole climbing ethos here plugs into an earlier style of risk and commitment. Many of the climbs are trash in modern terms, let's face it, but even these can generate big feelings and the warm glow of the full-blown epic. Like how you don't solo Everest for the moves.

The subtle things mean as much as the big things, the smell of salt in the spray, the little ironstone whirls captured in the rock like frozen waves. But so much of the climbing is a tactile response. Feel that edge, compress the rock like a spring between your four points of contact and burst yourself loose for the next hold. Try and smother or cuddle an arete like a big, rocky teddy bear.

Surprisingly there actually are some pleasant and safe climbs here. Diamond Bay has all the accoutrements of the sea cliffs (exposure, fear, poxy rock) without you having to die for your art. Start here and work downwards.

Mike Law

Above *Greg James.*
Opposite *Catherine Destivelle,* Clocks *(22).*
Following pages *Greg James,* The Bolt Ladder *(22).*

THE WARRUMBUNGLES

In a worn, flattened landscape like Australia, cliffs, gorges and other places of great physical relief stand out as impressive. But usually even if there's a hard way to the top, there's also an easy way. Nine times out of ten you can also walk . . . if not drive. Not in the Warrumbungles.

Towering over the north-western plains of New South Wales, this gathering of ancient volcanic plugs has captured human imagination for centuries. But it took three expeditions over five years for Australia's first mountaineers — Dr Dark and Dot Butler (nee English) — to finally unlock the secrets of the sharpest spire, Crater Bluff, in 1936. Like its neighbour, Belougery Spire, this is a summit which forces respect — the privilege of its views are only earned by unnatural moonlight starts and hours of continuous climbing, finishing in spindly ridges with the valley's trees reduced to grass-stems a thousand feet beneath your feet. For climbers, this kind of scale means many things.

It means perseverance beyond just physical strength. The first big route on Bluff Mountain — *Elijah*, a dozen pitches and Australia's most outrageous hand traverse — took Bryden Allen and partners eight days in 1964. Too weathered to carry chalk, it must still be tackled by forging a line as if the sleeping monster had never been climbed.

It means a whole new dimension in the lessons of height. Next door, on *Ginsberg*, Warwick Baird once slipped and took a 25-metre fall . . . still finishing up a good 200 metres clear of the ground and, apart from concussing his partner, none the worse for wear. Or to the left, *Flight of the Phoenix* sweeps out to a point where you lose all sense of exactly when you left the ground, or where you might find the top. You only reconnect to the world when you hear the sound of ruffling feathers and find yourself looking down onto the yellow-black of eagles' wings.

It means loving the dark — either the cool brush of invisible cypresses and grass trees on an alpine start, or a parched descent by moonlight. In these mountains the challenge of fighting gravity becomes entwined with others — the approach, the heat, the thirst, the shortness of the day, the infinite expanses of the rock — and the knowledge that you may well be tamed by defeat. It is a place where the urge to summit is spiced by the fact that retreats are twice as scary as finishing the climb; a landscape where the human ego is meaningless. A place owned, and retained, by the spirits.

AJ Brown

Above *Belougery Spire (left) and The Bread Knife.*
Opposite *Luchas Trihey (top) and Peter Jacobs,* Cornerstone Rib *(14, 190 metres), Crater Bluff.*

Right *AJ Brown (leading) and Jacob Greber,* Flight of the Phoenix *(18, 330 metres), Bluff Mountain.*

BOOROOMBA ROCKS

One thing you can't help noticing at Booroomba is the smallness of the holds. Somehow this seems unfair, because in every other respect the scale of the place is big. When you hike up through the tall forest on the back side of the ridge and arrive at the cliff top, the expansive view includes Canberra's glinting artificial lakes and its blight of suburbs, but dominating all is the imposing North Buttress.

NEW SOUTH WALES

Canberra • Sydney
Booroomba Rocks

And yet when you hit the cliffs, the holds are tiny — which, as it turns out, is perfect. The best climbing areas are those where the rock has been shaped by the cosmic architect to fit the needs of the human form stretched to its limit. Booroomba is at its most memorable when you find yourself fondling a crystal between thumb and index finger a long way above your protection. You squeeze the crystal, trying to make it grow in the way that a nipple sometimes does. A desperate person will try anything . . .

Your mouth is dry from remembering the little brass RP you semi-placed 15 metres below. You manage to reach a sharp edge which is enough to mantle on because the slab lays back from the vertical. Then you stand in balance with plenty of time to consider the deepness of the shit into which

you have gotten yourself. There is nowhere to go but up, another ten unprotected metres. You calm yourself, relatively speaking, and step off the last foothold between you and the end of the pitch. As you move up, intensity is tweaked to the limits of the dial. You make it, of course, but only because the alternative is unthinkable.

If your dance is with death, then leads like *Jubilate*, *Steele Breeze* and *Immaculate Deception* await you, hangovers from the Booroomba ethic of the 1970s when bolts were scorned. For the sane there are superb, sustained multi-pitch routes adequately protected by bolts and natural gear. Although an ocean of granite surrounds you on the vast slabs of the North Buttress, the rock can be friendly if you tune into its subtleties and know your limits. Booroomba's whitewater equivalents are the steep, sharp, modern routes on Snickers Wall, left of the central slabs, while on the South Buttress, *Integral Crack* is to me the river of life. The guide book will tell you the routes with stars, and as you'd expect there are plenty of them, given that granite is the rock of the gods. Booroomba is a great place to offer yourself, and to be reborn.

Lincoln Hall

Above *The North Buttress.*
Opposite *Tara Sutherland,* Integral Crack *(19), South Buttress.*

Opposite *Paul Cuthbert,* Teenage Wasteland *(25), South Buttress.*

Above *Nathan Wales, pitch three (21)* Nothing Left *(23, 135 metres), Central Slabs.*

Above *Chris Warner, pitch four (22)* Space
Wasted *(23, 155 metres), Central Slabs.*

Left *Rich Emmerson,* Global Gas Oven
(26), Snickers Wall.

Opposite *Justin Ryan,* Boy's Brigade
(25), Snickers Wall.

Frog Buttress

Here I am again, splayed and shaking, and my nemesis snapping at my ankles. Ten years ago, at this same move, I scoffed at low runners and lurched up, but mysterious powers sent me down, and my ankle snapped. So now, barely two metres off the ground, I herd my right toe back into the flake it seems to hate so much but at once it resumes its exasperating creep across the wall. The tendons in my groin stretch tauter still and shiver on their bones. I flick nervously at the crack with an RP and glance up the looming open groove. A rhyolyte book is propped above me — some distracted giant's slender tome, opened and abandoned to the vagaries of time, and I but an insect in the margin.

QUEENSLAND

Brisbane

Warwick

Frog Buttress

The crudely stacked pillars of Frog Buttress jut from the canopy of Mount French and bring to mind the haphazard shelves of some huge and ancient library. Its decaying volumes are forgotten by the giants, read now only by human insects that twitch across the pages, squeezing into the cracks, and floating down on rainbow threads. Here are books that will swallow you whole, a chorus of cicadas shrilling your requiem. For the passer by, the only evidence of your existence will be a dull clanking and the exhausted warthog grunts seeping from the depths of the crag. There are books that will burn you — their golden pages' perfect parabolas have focused the sun solely on the cremation of your flesh. And there are books that will seduce you, leading you jam by perfect jam, hand over hand

to a secret breezy eyrie. Who can now decipher what these pages promised in eons past?

A million Queensland suns have deconstructed the flaking lichened text, patiently levered off the words one by one, and clattered them into the forested scree beneath. We modern silverfish inch up the remnant dilapidated braille, scuttling and falling, and yet eke out a curious satisfaction. Each new climber fits the tiny orange edges, chalk flared jams, and spooky broken wires to a new reading.

My ankle intact, I pursue this garbled sentence, edge further up the pages, finding my security in the gutter margin, and then baulking at the tufted ends of a long weathered wire of history, I creep on by and scuttle into the belay. This time I've read the book unscathed. Did the ghosts of dead giants smile on me, or was the rumor true that ten years ago it had been my belayer that had wireguided me onto the only sharp rock below?

Roger Bourne

Above *Goanna.*
Opposite *Geoff Little,* Insomnia *(22).*

71

Top left and right *Geoff Little*, Insomnia *(22).*

Above left *Adam Donahue*, Guns of Navarone *(23).*

Above right *Tim Balla*, Satanic Majesty *(23).*

Opposite *Adam Donahue*, Impulse *(24).*

GIRRAWEEN

Nestled neatly into the hills of the Great Dividing Range, Girraween National Park is on the border of Queensland and New South Wales. The coarse granite — Stanthorpe Adamellite — exhibits a unique beauty. Throughout the year majestic displays of wildflowers give the area its name — Girraween means, in Aboriginal, 'place of the flowers'.

High on the ridges, precariously balanced boulders overlook open woodlands and meadows. Large tors, mammoth blocks of stone and scattered domes dominate the landscape. In the crook of steep-sided hills and hidden gorges, fern gullies quietly hide in cool damp retreats where lyrebirds vigorously sing.

The landscape resembles prehistoric shapes and forms, ancient tombs, ruins and monuments, invoking names such as the Pyramids and the Sphinx for these and similar areas. Cracks, flakes, aretes, walls and slabs unlock some of their hidden treasures.

Known to the local Kambwal tribe as Terrawambella, the Pyramids are a major feature in the park. In the 1960s Richard Sullivan and Robert Staszewski established the first major line on the second (Bald) Pyramid with the time-proven classic slab and flake of *Rourke's Rift*.

In the 1970s Henry Barber freed the beautifully named *Late Afternoon Flake* and Tobin Sorenson and John Allen freed one of the best lines in Queensland with *Scimitar*. Resembling the single-edged curve of a sword, this flake is clearly visible from the top of the first Pyramid. More recently some of the best include the wildly steep and sustained *New Paths*, the unrelenting arete of *Sheer Mettle*, and the elegant pocketed face of *It Takes a Thief*. Many routes are still being led, on sight, ground up, requiring commitment and determination. The crystal-pulling excursion of *Visible Speech*; the run-out and exhilarating *Not Safe, Slack!*; and the mind-blowing three-pitch adventure *Energizer* are but a few in this style.

With many climbing areas becoming over-utilised, bludgeoned and threatened by over-eager and thoughtless actions, efforts are being made to reduce this impact. Many major features and sensitive areas have been left untouched, or free of fixed protection, while their use is avoided in other areas unless there is no alternative. It is this minimalist approach which makes Girraween the climbing experience that it is.

And as the sun's last rays rest their softening touch on the landscape you should find a unique and fragile area, an area of mystery and discovery.

QUEENSLAND

Brisbane
Warwick

Girraween

Scott Camps

Above *Kookaburra.*
Opposite *Scott Camps,* New Paths *(24),* Turtle Rock.

Above *Balancing Rock on the First Pyramid.*

Right *Adam Donahue,* Alex in Wonderland *(23), Sphinx Rock.*

Below *Scott Camps,* Black Wall *(20), Sphinx Rock.*

Following pages *Scott Camps looking for a variant to* Late Afternoon Flake *(14), The Second Pyramid.*

MOONARIE

Like all the best climbing areas, Moonarie draws out both the spiritual and physical aspects of climbing. Before you even start climbing, Moonarie begins testing your resolve — the drive from Adelaide is a nightmare if the kangaroos are out, and the campsite desolate. The cliffs, set on the rim of Wilpena Pound in the dry heart of the Flinders Ranges, loom dispassionately over every step of the 40-minute uphill trudge to their base. The walk ends at Top Camp — a flat rock that towers over the plains from which you emerged and cowers under the cliffs that have drawn you.

Moonarie is at its best from Top Camp, it is here that the cliff's isolation, age and grandeur first invade your soul.

To the south of Top Camp is Checkers Wall, a layering of sunny orange faces sprinkled with cracks and roofs. The archetypal climb of the pioneering 1970s is here: the 120 metre *Pine Crack* — a direct cliff-splitting crack with long, sustained pitches and, of course, a roof.

The Gothic architecture of the Ramparts, on Top Camp's shady northern side, is one of Moonarie's greatest assets. Recessed faces, swollen buttresses, roofs, cracks, chimneys and corners all combine to give a spectacle as intimidating as it is alluring. The 1980s brought a new style of climb to Moonarie. With all the major weaknesses climbed, the new wave of developers turned to the features looming between cracklines. *Ape and Away*, *Endless Love*, and *Goblin Mischief* — long, single pitches to rap stations, combining perfect moves with exposure and commitment — are typical of this new style.

Around the corner from the Ramparts is the Great Wall, a 50 metre wall of outstanding beauty and quality. This popular wall is home to over a dozen 'three star' face climbs, among which *Downwind of Angels* and *Rip Off* are two of the finest for their grade anywhere.

Climbing at Moonarie is special. It's not just that the climbs approach perfection, it's the whole experience. For me this is the acuteness of the contradicting emotions — humility, euphoria, pride, shame — that make climbing, all climbing, so paradoxical. A paradox that no amount of thought or words can explain. A scratch that finds its only relief when I am caressing the stone of the Ramparts, or merely watching the eagles cruising the thermals above Moonarie Gap — just as they've done for thousands of years, and will be doing long after the stories of our conquests have been forgotten.

Stuart Williams

Sequence (bottom to top) Brent Hartshorne, Downwind of Angels *(19), The Great Wall.*
Opposite *Chad Harder,* Acid Rain *(24), Checkers Wall.*

Left Rob Baker, Goblin Mischief *(23)*, The Ramparts.

Above Brent Hartshorne, Cypress Avenue *(18)*, The Great Wall.

Above left Erika Zettervall, Outside Chance *(16)*, *The Great Wall.*

Above right Chad Albinger, Against the Wind *(23)*, *The Great Wall.*

Below Chad Harder, Icarus *(19)*, *The Ramparts.*

Above Breakfast time at Top Camp.

Below Sunrise from Top Camp.

BEN LOMOND

A vast plateau, and Tasmania's most dominant landform, with a cliff-girt escarpment of 30 or 40 kilometres, Ben Lomond is a peerless wilderness climbing area in the north-east of the state — a world apart. It is a mysterious place to most Australian climbers, of baffling complexity and size. There are no guidebooks — apart from various bits and pieces of old handwritten notes to the Northern Escarpment.

The rock is dolerite, that ubiquitous building material of Tasmanian tectonics. Magnificent to climb on, hard and with perfect friction, dolerite takes many forms, most of which can be encountered on the Ben. It's hard to believe that the massive sheared-off face at Heimdall on the Western Escarpment is the same rock as the severely regular columns of Frew's Flutes on the Northern Escarpment and Pavement Bluff on the Eastern Escarpment. On the Ben you can get some of the best face climbing around, as well as crack climbing of such quality it must have been conceived in heaven.

The climbing is special and so is the landscape. No-one leaves unaffected by the rare power of the high plateau, especially if they venture away from the easily accessed Northern Escarpment and wander down the broad wind-washed, sunwashed glacial valleys of the upland, along the shores of the high lakes to the bastions of Africa (Heimdall and Asgard), the columns of Pavement Bluff trapping the sun on the eastern rim or the darker labyrinthine towers and faces of Denison Crag and Stacks Bluff in the south.

Climbing first began on the Southern Escarpment. The first few tentative ascents were done at Stacks Bluff in 1971, but it is doubtful if climbing would have ever taken off in any major way had not the Northern Escarpment been 'discovered' in 1972. The golden years were the 1970s and early 1980s when the majority of the routes on the mountain were established. The cliffs were popular then and many overseas and visiting Australian climbers have the fondest memories of those years as well as a swag of first ascents.

Ben Lomond has never attracted climbers in any numbers. It is probably less popular today than it ever has been and climbing on the mountain is still like being in an era before there were climbers.

Robert McMahon

Above *Frew's Flutes.*
Opposite *Roxanne Wells,* Defender of the Faith *(21), Frew's Flutes.*

Top and right *Adam Donahue,*
Powerdive Direct *(22),* Frew's Flutes.

Above *Robert McMahon,* Sirocco *(21),*
Pavilion.

Frenchmans Cap

Frenchmans Cap — a proud white quartzite monolith rearing its head into the gales of the roaring forties. You sit in the rain-lashed hut, recovering from the ten-hour slog into Lake Tahune. The wind roars down from the North Col, and the pandanus rustle and knock like triffids.

When the sun shines though, it is a wild and awe-inspiring place to be. You wake to a breathless, pristine morning, and make your way up to the base of your route under a sky that seems to promise to stay blue forever. Three hundred and fifty metres of vertical and overhanging quartzite roars into the deep silent sky, its white rock dazzling in the light of the early morning. Your guts are in a knot, and your fingers sweat and tingle. The mountain is silent apart from the occasional lonely call of the currawong; your partner the only witness to your expletives and allusions to religion.

You wonder how those early ascensionists must have felt, launching up there in the 1960s with nothing better than a few machine nuts, slings and pegs in their technological arsenal. Even with modern equipment the rock can be difficult to protect. It can be a lonely place out there on the sharp end of the rope — no chalked holds to follow, no-one to tell you how to do the moves, no bolts to clip, and no rescues if you mess up.

Not everybody succeeds here. Usually it's the weather. Sometimes it's intimidation. Sometimes the void simply sucks insidiously away at your resolve until even the cockiest climber is reduced to a snivelling mamma's boy. As Doug Fife said during our retreat down acres of steep, black rock after an attempt on the roofs of Tahune Face: 'I just want a big fat nipple to suck on.'

You walk out, swearing and cursing every time you slip, trip or stumble over the wet roots or through the knee-deep mud. But after your body has stopped aching, after your mind has recovered from the psychological stress of the climbing, what you remember is half-a-dozen of the best moments in a climber's life — the long exposed traverse; your heart in your mouth as you launch up a wildly overhanging pitch 200 metres off the deck; or the exquisite climbing on a sunny piece of rock way above a shadowy void, hidden somewhere around the back of the mountain. That's when you start thinking about the next route you're going to do there . . .

Peter Steane

Above *The East Face.*
Opposite *Eric Morlino, pitch three* Tierry le Fronde *(17, 145 metres), Tahune Face.*

Top left David Jenkins crossing the Franklin River at the start of the 25-kilometre walk to Tahune Hut.

Top right Discovering why the Lodden Plains are also called the 'Sodden Lodden'.

Above left Day two of the walk in, with Garn Cooper in front, and Barren Pass in the background.

Above right Garn Cooper belaying, pitch four The Ninth of January.

Above left *Garn Cooper, pitch two* The Ninth of January *(19, 160 metres), East Face.*

Above right *David Jenkins, pitch three* The Ninth of January.

Freycinet Peninsula

This is a separate world . . . a paradise — and not just for climbers. The Freycinet Peninsula extends south into the Tasman Sea for over 30 kilometres out from the east coast of Tasmania. A soft coastal mildness sets it apart from other Tasmanian climbing areas.

The Hazards dominate first impressions, dramatically rising above the holiday resort of Coles Bay. Seen from there, in the full blast of the sun, they can appear as a chaos of granite. Some cliffs stand out — Mount Amos catches the early sun, which highlights its facetted surface. It was here, and on the neighbouring Sow Spur, that serious climbing first began in the late 1960s. Runout slabs abound, and cracks come in many forms, including carnivorous offwidths. Finely textured grey intrusions give delight amongst the coarse pink crystals. High on Amos there is polished smoothness which reflects the sun like glass. Between the major cliffs lie endless boulders and craglets; concentrated quality with idiosyncratic challenges, like the overhanging prows of Gracelands. The individual areas are extensive, but their proximity convenient. One can leave a climb and cross the valley to an entirely different cliff, several times a day.

Out of sight to the east is a deeply incised coastline, where Freycinet's most popular area is hidden. White Water Wall was opened up in the 1970s, and so started the coastal climbing scene. It now sports the easiest, safest, and hardest routes. The three kilometres from here to Cape Tourville is an extremely beautiful environment for all kinds of activities, having comfortable access to zawns, stacks and walls. The often spectacular routes are usually one pitch, on superb grey granite, and in close proximity to a dramatic sea presence. Stunning rock architecture, and tranquil scenery add to the attraction.

Cape Tourville overlooks the indigo shadows of Sleepy Bay. Then starts the great sweep of Hazards Main Wall. Climbing here is on a larger scale and more serious, with slabs rising over 300 metres. The base provides one of Australia's unique traverses which extends over two kilometres and involves a swim — the *Sea Level Traverse*. Half way along, are some of the peninsula's greatest jewels. Firstly, the Gonk, a defiant prow of provocative architecture, and then the big curve of Flow Stone Wall. This is home to daringly unprotected slab routes of the early 1980s. It is heroic country — long, lonely and remote.

Scenic beauty attracts everyone to Freycinet, while the diverse possibilities for climbers make it an essential part of the Tasmanian experience.

Peter Jackson

Above *The Hazards from the township of Coles Bay.*
Opposite *Roxanne Wells,* Beowulf *(17), Deepwater Zawn.*

Opposite *Roxanne Wells,* Apline *(13), White Water Wall.*

Above left *Grant Rowbottom,* Via Magna *(27), The Underworld.*

Above right *Grant Rowbottom,* Exquisite Tenderness *(28), Alchemy Wall.*

Above *Grant Rowbottom*, Via Magna *(27)*, The Underworld.   ***Opposite*** *David Jones*, Kodak Tart *(26)*, White Stack.

Left *David Jenkins*, Don't Land on the Lunch *(19)*, Hazards Main Wall.

Right *Roxanne Wells*, Light Fingered Maddison *(20)*, near White Water Wall.

Below *Donna Bridge*, The Horizontal Chimney *on the* Sealevel Traverse *(16)*.

MOUNT WELLINGTON

Mount Wellington looms above Hobart like some dark monolith. In the depths of winter it is plastered with snow like a giant iced cake, in summer its purple hue seems an adaptation of the sky — airy, ethereal, unreal. Always, the jagged line of the Organ Pipes stands out, as clear as a character-creating scar on an otherwise ordinary face.

The Organ Pipes is the main climbing cliff on Mount Wellington. There are other areas — Lost World, New World, Sphinx Rock — but the Pipes is the longest, highest and most atmospheric cliff of them all. Even on a summer's day when there are other climbers around, being on one of the many multi-pitch routes fills you with a sense of grandeur, height and aloneness. Voices and the clanking of gear are echoed and amplified, making people seem closer than they really are, but this is a place where the sky becomes subsumed by cliff, and dolerite thrusts endlessly up into the blue.

Nothing seems to match the height, the exposure and the sense of being so far above the rest of the world, as well as that stillness and silence of the Pipes. It's as though even the wind has stopped to listen. On misty days you can climb in a sea of cloud with Hobart materialising beneath your feet only occasionally — a strange, other-worldly sensation.

Climbing first began on the Pipes in the 1960s, although it was fairly slow and haphazard progress. Activity increased in the 1970s with development spreading to all sections of the cliff. If there is any one style that defines climbing on the Pipes, it is jamming up the abrasive cracks and off-widths between the soaring dolerite columns. However, there are many hundreds of climbs

and a range of styles: traditional cracks and corners, and more extreme, bolted faces and aretes. But whether crack, corner, face, arete, traditional or new, no single climb can define the Pipes.

The Pipes are huge, towering cliffs that emphasise your smallness and mortality, scree slopes that seem to descend all the way to the Derwent River, spongy, sharp pineapple grass, blocks of dolerite, flakes, cracks and faces, amphitheatres and buttresses, flanges and pinnacles, ankle-twisting rocks, long, steep descent routes, endless abseils, tea tree, stunted eucalypts and, always, columns of sheer rock, achingly high above Hobart.

Adrienne Eberhard

Above *The Organ Pipes on Mount Wellington, above Hobart.*
Opposite *Steve Monks,* After Midnight *(23), Flange Buttress.*

Above *Roger Parkyn,* In Flagrante Delicto *(24),* The Amphitheatre.

Opposite *Sam Edwards,* Pleasant Screams *(26),* Flange Buttress.

TASMAN PENINSULA

The strikingly slender 65-metre dolerite column which is the Totem Pole holds an iconic appeal to any climber. It stands close enough to the mainland for one to be able throw stones at its summit — tantalisingly close — yet its staunch posture and uncompromising surroundings give rise to a feeling of dread.

My ascent of the original aid route with Steve Bunton started badly when we poked our noses over the cliff edge. The churning waters at the base looked like grade five kayaking material. The only alternative to turning back there and then was an old rope linking the mainland to the first belay. It had been flapping about in the breeze for a few years, the sheath was worn through in several places, but there was enough of the inner stringy stuff left for me to pull across, nervously, and get established.

The rest of the ascent didn't exactly go smoothly either. Both of us took falls and a cheatstick, kindly left on the first belay, was used more than once. The dubious tactics we'd used, however, didn't stop us being rapt when we got to the top! An awesome place to be. It was an ascent that took all the commitment that a pair of average aid climbing bumblies, such as ourselves, could muster.

More recently I was fortunate enough to climb the *Free Route* with Sam Edwards. It is an exceptional addition. The Totem Pole is still a formidable challenge and nature's kindness is essential for any ascent. A cold wind, sea spray and shivering belayers add to the difficulty and a high swell often makes it impossible even to start. It is telling that, in the three summers since the *Free Route* was done, it has still not had a repeat ascent in true 'free' style.

The Totem Pole is not the only worthwhile climbing objective in the area. The overhanging sport climbing at the Paradiso provides a welcome change from the vertical crack climbing more typically found in Tasmania; the swim through shark-infested waters to the Candlestick provides a psychological challenge reminiscent of scampering under ice cliffs on an alpine ascent; Mount Brown contains some awesome multi-pitch routes and the Moai has an eclectic style all of its own.

Perhaps the climbing on the Tasman Peninsula is characterised more by the feeling of remoteness, the beauty of the surroundings and the presence of the sea than any unifying feature of the climbing itself.

Roger Parkyn

Above *Steve Monks starts up the Totem Pole for the first free ascent. Jane Wilkinson gets drenched.*
Opposite *Steve Monks, pitch one* The Free Route *(25), The Totem Pole, Cape Hauy.*
Pitches are 25 and 25.

Above *The 65-metre Totem Pole, with the mainland to the right and*
The Candlestick to the left.

Opposite *Simon Mentz, pitch two* The Free Route *(25),* The Totem Pole.

Opposite *Jane Wilkinson and Steve Monks on the half-way ledge, with Simon Mentz climbing below.*

Top left *Simon Mentz, following pitch one* The Free Route *(25), the Totem Pole.*

Top right *Adam Darragh using a Tyrolean traverse to access the Totem Pole.*

Above left *Jane Wilkinson starting across the Tyrolean traverse.*

Above right *Simon Carter (left), Simon Mentz and Jane Wilkinson ride home from Cape Hauy.*

Opposite *Sam Edwards,* Sacred Site *(18),* The Moai.

Above left and right *Sam Edwards,* Thunderbirds Are Go *(24),* The Paradiso.

THE GRAMPIANS

Basking in the heart of Victoria's Western District are a series of saw-tooth mountains that radiate outwards like the spokes of a buckled bicycle wheel. These are the Grampians and many argue that no other area in the country can match the rich diversity of its climbing, nor the quality of its rock. Despite having played second fiddle to nearby Mount Arapiles for many years, this extensive range is capturing the attention of climbers now more than ever. Its hundreds of cliffs include severely overhanging orange walls, sweeping escarpments and isolated towers. It is a region that promises new cliffs and new climbs for generations to come.

It was as a brash young whippersnapper that I experienced my first climbing adventure in the Grampians. A friend and I thrashed our way up *Mixed Climb*, which at grade 12 is one of the easiest routes on Mount Rosea. Assuming it to be a doddle, we were somewhat shocked to encounter steep, exposed and intricate climbing on every one of its five pitches. But this is exactly what makes Grampians sandstone so special — whatever your ability, it offers thought-provoking and varied climbing for all.

In recent years, I've had the privilege of witnessing some of the Grampian's more remarkable and overhanging architecture succumb to legendary strongman Malcolm Matheson. One memorable occasion involved a group of us exploring a large unclimbed cave deep in the heart of the Victoria Range. While the rest of the group contemplated piddly little routes on the fringes, Malcolm pointed out a line that went across the entire roof — a full 50 metres! Although we all scoffed at his proposal, he proved us wrong, not only by climbing the thing, but by doing it entirely without bolts. Malcolm's ascent of *Welcome to Barbados* joined a long list of celebrated test pieces already bearing his name.

Climbing in the Grampians isn't always hassle free: dusty roads; suicidal 'roos that insist on leaping in front of your vehicle; scrub-bashing approaches that begin to feel like the dying days of a Burke and Wills expedition. But then there are those crags that require only five minute walk-ins, offer convenient camping caves, and surrounding flora and fauna which is just as fascinating as the climbing. And with everything from trad routes, sport routes, remote adventure routes and bouldering to choose from, well . . .what more could you ask for?

Simon Mentz

Above *Koala, in-situ near Taipan Wall.*
Opposite *Andrew Dunbar, pitch two (crux) Serpentine (29), Taipan Wall.*

Sequence (from left to right) *Malcolm Matheson,* Mirage *(27),*
Taipan Wall. Motor drive at 3.6 frames per second.

Following pages *Taipan Wall, Mount Stapylton.*

Opposite *Stuart Wyithe, pitch two (28)* Cardigan Street *(31),*
Taipan Wall.

Above *David Jones,* Milupa *(28),* Wall of Fools, *Summer Day Valley.*

Right *David Jones,* One Bed to the Left *(27), Cliche Wall.*

Left *Bobbi Bensman,* Monkey Puzzle *(28), The Gallery.*

Above *Kennan Harvey,* Pythagoras' Theorem *(26), Eureka Wall.*

Opposite *Steve Monks,* Pythagoras' Theorem *(26), Eureka Wall.*

Below *Julian Saunders,* Le Petit Mort *(29), The Gallery.*

Following pages *Julian Saunders,* Shattering Reflections of Narcissism *(29), Millennium Caves.*

Opposite and above *Julian Saunders,* Shattering Reflections of
Narcissism *(29),* Millennium Caves.

Left and above Malcolm Matheson,
Welcome to Barbados *(29), Red Cave.*
A 50 metre climb finishing through the
left-hand window in the photograph above.

Above and right *Jill McLeod and Kirsty Hamilton belaying, pitch two (crux)* Passport to Insanity *(27), The Fortress.*

MOUNT ARAPILES

To climbers the name 'Arapiles' has magical, almost mythical, qualities — no doubt as the name *Djurid* had for its earlier inhabitants. Geological time has been gentle on the rock of Arapiles, eroding the surrounding plains yet leaving this escarpment standing proud. The continual harshness of nature has enriched its texture, not marred it. It has produced a myriad of cracks, holds, faces, gullies and the best runner placements in Australia.

The rock is hard. It is round and smooth, offering at times no friction to your skating feet or desperately slapping hand. But the holds and gear are good. Other cliffs may have their own nature but Arapiles' strength is its sheer variety. The character of the crag, with its million-plus holds, has produced some 3000 routes. There are some of the best easy or beginner routes in the world: *Arachnus*; *Siren*; the immortal *Bard;* and most of the climbs in the Organ Pipes. User-friendly as the lower grade

climbs are, as you progress through the grades other aspects of Arapiles routes become apparent, particularly their ability to render your arms unto mud in next to no time at all.

There are slabs like the elegant *Brolga* and the exquisitely thin *Auto Da Fe*; roofs to play on like the toy *Pilot Error* and the much coveted and photographed *Kachoong*. There are walls, offwidths, handcracks, face climbs, jumps, chimneys, squeezes, doddles and desperates. There are so many fine routes at almost any grade, test pieces such as *Little Thor*, *Los Endos*, *Anxiety Neurosis* and *Cobwebs*. And at the pinnacle of difficulty is Wolfgang Gullich's feat, the legendary *Punks in the Gym*.

As fine as all the mountain's classic routes are, for many people, including me, Arapiles' most precious quality is not the rock itself but the whole experience — its history of epics, remarkable feats of climbing, all-night parties; the natural environment, a place that is both beautiful and humbling to experience, from still, mist-shrouded winter days to vivid autumn afternoon sunsets, from bouldering in rainy caves to sitting in the dust of the pines on a far too hot day; the friendliness of the crag, where everyone you pass will smile and nod, where conversations amongst the boulders or rides back from the pub are as easy to arrange as a hot shower isn't.

Arapiles. Djurid. It is one of a kind. A great cliff. Experience it. Treasure it.

Greg Pritchard

Above *Rest day in The Pines campground for Frey Yule and Kirsty McKenzie.*
Opposite *Simon Mentz,* The Prow *(27),* Bluff Major.

Top *Bobbi Bensman bouldering.*

Above *Frey Yule bouldering.*

Right *Canola transforms a Wimmera paddock.*

Left *Anna Jansen*, Missing Link *(17)*, Bluff Major.

Above *Abby Watkins*, The Low Down *(25)*, Castle Crag.

Above *Paul Deacon*, Muldoon *(13)*, The Atridae.

Below *David Jones*, Punks in the Gym *(32)*, The Pharos.

Previous pages *Venus Kondos,* Kachoong *(21), The Northern Group.*

Above left *Louise Shepherd, pitch five* Bard *(12, 120 metres), Bard Buttress.*

Above right *Felicity Butler,* Thunder Crack *(21), Bluff Major.*

Opposite *Ian Vickers,* Ethiopia *(30), The Pharos. A continuation of* India *(28).*

Left *Andy Pollitt rapping off Castle Crag.*

Above (from top) *Volker Jurisch at Mitre Billabong; Frey Yule's rest day, complete with a comfy chair and good book; a kangaroo in Central Gully finds it all quite curious.*

Above (from top) *A view from Mitre Rock; Mount Arapiles reflections; star trails for four and a half hours over The Bluffs.*

Right *Dawn on Bard Buttress with Castle Crag and Mitre Rock in the background.*

Above *Stuart Lourding, The Watchtower Crack (16, 100 metres), The Watchtower.*

Right *Dave Musgrove, Los Endos (22), Wind Wall.*

MOUNT BUFFALO

Every summer since I started climbing I've made the annual pilgrimage to Buffalo. And still, every summer, I look forward to going back. The long drive across flat, dry plains which seem to go on forever until you finally see Buffalo and the surrounding Alps rising huge and blue on the distant horizon. That first sight of the gorge cleaving deeply into the eastern rim of the plateau a thousand metres above you. And the slow, stomach-churning crawl up the twisting road to the plateau.

Every year I head straight to the gorge to see, as if for the first time again, the imposing 250-metre North Wall. This is the place which has most fired the imagination of climbers since they first began coming here back in the 1930s. Since the 1960s, when it was first climbed, it has been the birth place of many classic big wall aid climbs. Summer and winter ascents, single and multi-day, desperate epics and grand adventures, the North Wall has seen them all. Routes such as *Ozymandias*, *Lord Gumtree*, *Emperor* and *Fuhrer* were hammered in the 1960s, nutted in the 1970s and, some of them, finally, freed in the 1980s and 1990s. And it still continues to attract aspiring hard men and women who are keen to pay their big wall dues.

Then it's up to the high plateau, mentally making a list of all the old and new classics I want to do. The Cathedral, The Hump, Dreamworld, The Horn — where to start? Cracks, faces, slabs or aretes? Long or short? Moderate or hard? It doesn't really matter because there are so many to choose from and they all have that magic ingredient — coarse, crystalline granite with the kind of friction that seems to defy the laws of physics. Granted, some cracks do require heavy taping in order to avoid drawing blood. But it's also possible to spend an entire summer at Buffalo without inserting any part of you into anything more rugged than an armchair in the Chalet lounge.

Albury–Wodonga

Mount Buffalo

VICTORIA

Melbourne

But one of the things I love most about Buffalo is, like all great climbing areas, there is far more on offer than just rock. Fragile meadows filled with wildflowers and weathered granite tors, surrounded by snow gums and criss-crossed by crystal-cold mountain streams. The cool waters of Lake Catani soothing shredded skin and sore muscles as you dream away a hot afternoon far above the baking plains. Knowing next summer you'll be back to enjoy it all over again . . .

Kirsty Hamilton

Above *A damselfly pauses on candleheath.*
Opposite *Steve Monks, pitch six (28) Ozymandias Direct (28), The North Wall.*

Left *Enga Lokey, pitch two* Defender of the Faith *(23, 185 metres), North Wall.*

Above *The North Wall.*

Below *John Fantini (left) and Geoff Gledhill, fifth belay* Lord Gumtree *(M6, 22, 315 metres), The North Wall.*

Opposite *Malcolm Matheson,* Lebensraum *(25), The North Wall.*

Above (from left to right) *Steve Monks*, Ozymandias Direct, *pitch six (28).*

Opposite (from bottom to top) *Steve Monks*, Ozymandias Direct, *pitch two (28).*

Ozymandias Direct *is a 270-metre classic on The North Wall.*
Pitches are 22, 28, 26, 24, 22, 28, 23, and 24.

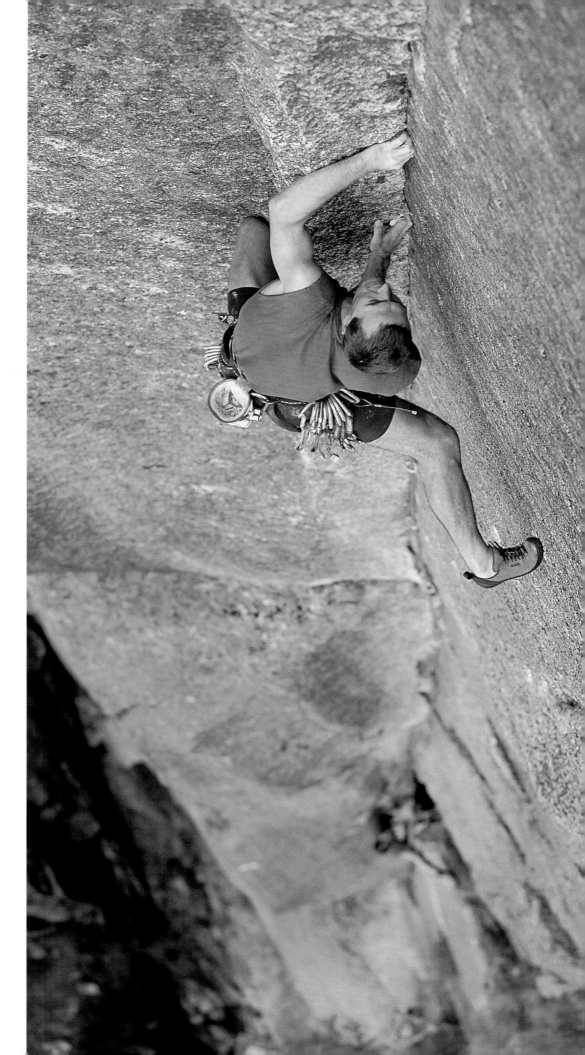

Opposite *Mark Baker,* Vanity Fair *(25), False Modesty Pinnacle.*

Above *Malcolm Matheson, project, False Modesty Pinnacle.*

Top left *The Plateau with (from left to right) The Horn, The Hump and The Cathedral.*

Top right *Enga Lokey atop The Cathedral.*

Above left *Vera Wong and John Fantini belaying, pitch two* Hard Rain *(22, 110 metres), The Gorge.*

Above right *Mark Davies and Mike Moore belaying, pitch two* Monarch *(22, 75 metres), The Gorge.*

Opposite *Steve Monks, pitch one* The Dreaming *(23, 90 metres), The Cathedral.*

Above *Gordon Brysland and Malcolm Matheson belaying, pitch two*
The Icing on the Cake *(22, 75 metres),* The Hump.

Right *Simon Thompson and Greg Moore belaying,* This Is Not Our
Land *(19), Dreamworld.*

Below *Simon Mentz,* Peroxide Blond *(20),* The Horn.

ALBANY

Sea cliff climbing around Albany is exciting, and the wider area is the most neglected vertical play-ground in Australia. It offers aesthetic masterpieces on Peak Head, exposed zawn horrors at The Gap, 10-pitch semi-alpine routes on Bluff Knoll, and funky dome excursions in the Porongurups.

WESTERN
AUSTRALIA

Perth

Albany

Peak Head offers long pitches far above a booming Southern Ocean on flawless fine-grained granite, all less than 30 minutes from the car. The clean rock features dictate a narrow-banding of grades from 15 to 22. Any modern hit-list should include *Albatross*, *Skysurfer* and *Power of the Old Land*. Peak Head is a slightly more mellow experience than mega-exposed venues like The Gap, but opportunities remain to 'push the boat out' on vast South Face expanses between established lines.

The Gap is a steep, committing paradise above the surging maelstrom . . . it makes *The Fear* seem like a kids' picnic. And tourist hordes carry on like hyenas waiting to capture your terrible plunge on video. Krakken-meister Kim Carrigan cleaned up most of the steep stuff back in 1986. Good ones include *Horrie on my Heels*, *Vee-Wheeze* and *Dampness at Noon*. But not everything here requires your will to be made before tying on. Shorter routes at Natural Bridge and the Amphitheatre are less stomach-turning but keep the basic theme.

Bluff Knoll is but one cliff in that vast cradle of West Australian climbing — the Stirling Range. At 1073 metres, the Bluff has suspect rock (always), route-finding nightmares (usually) and winter snow (sometimes). Extreme weather arrives without warning and tourist 'firing squads' may hurl toaster-sized rocks at you from the summit. Completed in 1972, *Coercion* opened an era of exploration, benightments and controversy. Modern testpieces include *Sophocles Pillar* and *Caveat Emptor*, both of which wink from the outer edges of seriousness. A free ascent of the *Great Roof Route* still awaits.

The Porongurups is a lesser range situated between the Stirling and the coast, offering mostly dome frolics on granite of variable quality. Gibraltar Rock, scene of the legendary 1974 ascent of *Dockyard Wall*, has the biggest and best lines. *Dinosaur*, *Joint Venture*, *Let the Fun Begin* and the recent creation *A Call to Arms* are all rip-snorters. Also in the Albany region is West Cape Howe — then there are the nearby wineries . . .

Gordon Brysland

Above Peak Head.
Opposite Joel Booth, Baylac Direct *(18)*, Peak Head

Opposite *Boyd MacNamara and Joel Booth belaying*, When the Horrie Cometh *(17)*, The Gap.

Above *Boyd MacNamara, bouldering at The Gap.*

KALBARRI

Over the centuries, the Murchison River has cut deeply into the plains to form a gorge which is engulfed by extraordinary sandstone and shale cliffs. The river slithers in the fashion of a snake, meandering between beautiful walls, which are mostly crumbly but joined by sections which are reliably compact. The climbing at Kalbarri can be found at crags that are about half an hour's drive from the town. The most prominent area is the Z-Bend, which has seen most of the development in recent years. Other areas include the D-Loop and Hawks Head.

The first recorded climbing at Kalbarri dates back to June 1985. This saw the establishment of arguably the most popular traditional climb of the region — *Keith Goes Blank* — which takes the most obvious crack line visible from the Z-Bend lookout. However it wasn't until the winters of 1993 and 1994 that Kalbarri was rediscovered as a popular climbing destination. In their desperation to find some of the much lacking steep rock in Western Australia, a dedicated group of friends set off on the seven-hour journey for Kalbarri. On arrival there were sighs of disappointment, but a 20-minute walk into the gorge from the Z-Bend lookout bore the most unexpected yet desirable fruit ever to be imagined. Steep, compact, and severely overhanging sandstone. A crag later to be known as the infamous Promenade.

From that day on, some of Western Australia's most difficult sport climbs were opened with the establishment of routes such as *Busting Down the Door*, *The Glass Slipper*, and *Jizz Lobber*. Other crags with a selection of traditional routes have also appeared in the Z-Bend area throughout the same period. Some of the more challenging of these are found in the Ravine, which as the name suggests, is a deep and narrow ravine enclosed by extremely compact and blank walls.

The Kalbarri climbing experience is more than just the climbing though, as the area is arguably limited in comparison to other Australian climbing destinations. There is the sheer beauty and tranquillity of the location. Being primarily a winter climbing destination, there is the silence of the perfect sunny day broken only by the sound of water flowing between the rocks. This is what will ensure that Kalbarri continues to be a prime climbing location in Western Australia.

Anthony Bell

Above *Kalbarri Gorge.*
Opposite *Anthony Bell,* Root Canal *(26),* The Promenade.

159

Opposite Chris Jones, Heavy Petting *(23)*, The Promenade.

Above Simon Birch, Root Canal *(26)*, The Promenade.

Below Emily Grigg, Rattler *(22)*, The Pit.

Above Chris Jones, Busting Down the Door *(27)*, The Promenade.

Right Anthony Bell, Heavy Petting *(23)*, The Promenade.

MARGARET RIVER

I first discovered the Margaret River area as an impressionable teenager escaping the city with my mates on our school holidays. We slept in our surfboard covers, ate two-minute noodles, prayed for waves and tried to convince girls from around the campfire to go for a 'walk' down the beach. Nowadays my thoughts of Margaret River have shifted towards a different focus; one that, while not necessarily more mature, is more associated with strong coffee and the buzz of my drill than the innocent pleasures of my youth. For me, climbing in this deeply forested coastal region is very much a part of the West Australian climbing experience.

In the past, climbing here has focused on the orange, curved gneiss that juts proudly from the Indian Ocean at Moses Rocks, Cosy Corner and Willyabrup. The latter is host to a superb and diverse range of climbs that take venerable lines up the numerous buttresses of this wave and windswept crag. Willyabrup is at its best with the salt spray from a thumping south-wester flicking across your neck as you reach tentatively around the lip on *One For the Road*, muscle your way up the underclinging *Mobjob* or perhaps try to unravel the secrets of *Heavy Metal*.

With the new trend towards supermarket-style cragging, these bastions of traditional climbing have now become as unfashionable as many old cliffs are these days apt to do. It seems holiday snaps of your friends are far more impressive when a cliff hangs ominously over you rather than sulking away in diminished slabfullness. With this in mind, the development of sport crags like Bob's Hollow and Wallcliffe has changed the very nature of Margaret River climbing. By opening a more diverse range of styles and rock, these tufa dripped and stalactite laden sweatfests entice the climber to *Bee Free*, and enjoy all the *Fun, Love and Joy* they can handle.

These limestone crags reflect the future of Margaret River climbing — with only a dozen of the 300 odd recorded formations across the whole region receiving any interest from climbers, there is plenty of rock still to be discovered. It is amazing that while development in this region had slowed to a crawl during the early 1990s, a change in attitudes and a little bit of vision has seen this area once again enter a period of growth.

Chris Jones

Above Glen Henderson, Willaybrup.
Opposite Amanda Watts, Dessert (24), Willyabrup.

Top and right *Amanda Watts*, Heavy Metal *(24), Willyabrup.*

Above middle *Chris Jones*, One For The Road *(19), Willyabrup.*

Above *Glen Henderson*, Delving Devoids *(25), Willyabrup.*

Left Anthony Bell, project, Bob's Hollow.

Above Chris Loane, Spatchula Man *(26)*, Bob's Hollow.

Below Gerard Chipper, Flight of the Intruder *(26)*, Golgotha Crag.

West Cape Howe

At the edge of a windswept peninsula 40 kilometres south-west of Albany lie the sea cliffs of West Cape Howe. This remote place has several kilometres of sea frontage only accessible by four-wheel drive through sand dunes and scrub. The battered cliffs face Antarctica — and for the climber taking on the added exposure of big waves and spray it can be a formidable experience.

The crags can be up to 70 metres high and while some areas are able to be walked into, many routes start from the bottom of an abseil — as close as one dares to the surging water. Either way, there is an amazing variety and quality of climbing to savour. Dolerite is the dominant rock and forms dark-coloured buttresses split with abundant cracks, flakes and zawns. Up close, the rock has a scaly texture like the skin of a giant reptile and exhibits just the right touch of friction.

Given that many walls are just under vertical and laden with features, intimidating lines are easier and often better protected than they first appear. There are slabs like *Nosewheel* and *Planar Craving* which rely on smearing and fine edging techniques to climb a reclined billiard table of stone hidden along Southern Ocean Wall; cracks to climb amidst a vertical landscape of square-edged pillars with routes like *The Climb* on the Old Man of Torbay sea-stack; and routes like *Gay Blade* and *Dreaded Lurgy* which are harder propositions up steeper angles and jutting edges.

WESTERN
AUSTRALIA

Perth

West Cape   Albany
Howe

Look out for loose blocks and decomposed rock in some places — stories of close shaves with rocks the size of refrigerators and chopped ropes are common. Another hazard is the sea — not so much when swells are high, as climbing then is usually out of the question. But it's the king waves on a calm day which take you by surprise, often surging up onto dry ledges and drenching unsuspecting belayers.

Like most big sea cliffs, West Cape Howe overwhelms the senses and makes you feel incredibly vulnerable. The rhythmic pounding of Southern Ocean swells against the base of the cliffs mixes with a strong scent of sea spray and heath. Dark grey walls with splashes of bright grey granite contrast with the vivid blue sea. It's a memorable atmosphere and if you're lucky a pod of whales might just cruise past.

David Wagland

Above *A wild frontier of land and sea.*
Opposite *Boyd MacNamara,* Trundle Fun *(19), Southern Ocean Wall.*

169

Left *Greg Mortimer and Pete Nidd belaying,* The Climb *(18),
Old Man of Torbay.*

Above *The West Cape Howe peninsula.*

Opposite *Boyd MacNamara,* Didi Wa Didi *(22), Reptilian Wall.*

Below *Gordon Brysland,* Rub and Tug *(19), Southern Ocean Wall.*

Following pages *Boyd MacNamara and Joel Booth belaying,* Acid
Drop *(17), Southern Ocean Wall.*

GLOSSARY

Abseil Method for descending a rope.

Aid Climbing Mechanically-assisted climbing. Body weight is supported by protection, or other devices, and these are used to directly 'aid' upwards progress.

Alpine climbing, Alpinism Climbing higher peaks or mountains, often involves climbing snow and ice.

Anchor Point where the rope is fastened to the rock.

Arete A jutting prow of rock, an outside corner.

Belay The system using a rope to arrest a climber's fall. Includes the anchors and stance that the 'belayer' uses, and involves using a friction (belay) device to lock-off the rope.

Big Wall A big cliff offering particularly long rock routes, possibly requiring numerous days to climb.

Bolt A construction bolt fixed into a pre-drilled hole as a permanent anchor or protection point.

Bouldering Unroped climbing close to the ground.

Buttress A large protuding section of cliff.

Cam, Camming unit Protection device that expands into a crack.

Carabiner, Karabiner Metal alloy snaplinks used to connect the rope to protection and anchor points.

Chalk Gymnasts chalk used to dry sweating fingertips for better grip.

Cheatstick Used in aid climbing; a stick or short pole used to clip the rope to out-of-reach protection points.

Choss Soft, loose, crumbly rock.

Chimney A body-sized crack, or bigger.

Crag A smaller cliff or set of cliffs.

Crux The most difficult section of the climb.

Face A steep open section of cliff.

Free, free climbing Climbing using hands and feet (and any other body parts) to climb the rock's natural features. The rope and protection are there, but are not used to 'aid' the ascent.

Flash To lead climb a route on the very first attempt but with some prior knowledge of the difficulties or sequence of moves.

Flake A semi-detached plate of rock.

Grade A subjective rating of the difficulties of the climb. There are different grading systems for aid climbs, free climbs, and boulder problems. See page 175 for comparisons with other countries' grading systems.

Ground-up To climb from ground level without previously inspecting or preparing the route. As opposed to 'top-down'.

Hawser-laid An old method of rope construction.

Hanging belay Where there is no ledge to use as a belay stance, the belayer sits in the harness suspended from the belay anchors.

Jam, Jamb A climbing technique where a hand or foot is squeezed inside a crack to provide a hold.

Jumar Brand of rope-ascending device which clamps around the rope and uses a metal tooth cam to stop it from sliding down. 'Jumaring' is a generic name for the technique of ascending fixed ropes.

Lead To climb up first from the ground, without a rope from above.

Multi-pitch A longer route which is climbed in sections (pitches).

Natural protection Non-permanent protection devices that can be easily placed and removed (not bolts or pitons).

Nut Metal wedge-shaped protection device that is inserted into cracks.

Offwidth A wide crack, awkward to climb.

On-sight An ethically pure free climbing style. The climb is lead climbed 'ground-up' on the first attempt, without any falls or pulling on gear, and without any prior knowledge of the moves.

Overhang A extra steep ('overhanging') section of rock.

Pitch A section of cliff which is climbed between belay points.

Piton (peg or pin) Metal protection device (hammered into cracks).

Port-a-ledge On long multi-day climbs without adequate sleeping ledges, climbers haul their own portable ledges up the cliff.

Project An attempted climb, not yet properly free climbed.

Protection The many different types of equipment attached to the rock as anchors to stop a falling climber. Includes camming devices, metal wedges (wires, nuts, RPs, stoppers and hexes), nylon slings, pitons and bolts.

Prusik, prussik To ascend a fixed rope using short loops of narrow rope tied around the main rope with a non-slip 'prusik' knot.

Pockets Holes in the rock face.

Quickdraw Two carabiners joined by a short nylon sling.

Rappel, rap To abseil.

Redpoint A style of climbing, widely regarded as the minimum ethical standard for a 'free' ascent. The route must be lead climbed without a fall or any assistance from the rope or protection.

Roof A horizontally-overhanging section of rock.

RP A brand of very small brass protection nuts.

Runner, running belay The protection point or anchor placed on the climb by the lead climber. The lead climber's rope 'runs' through a carabiner connected to the protection, hence 'runner'.

Runout The distance the lead climber is above their last piece of protection. A 'runout' climb is one with big fall potential.

Second The climber who ascends the pitch after the lead climber.

Slab A large off-vertical sheet of rock, often climbed with balance and friction techniques.

Solo To climb alone — in free climbing this means without a rope ('free solo'); in aid climbing a rope is used ('aid solo').

Sport climbing Where the emphasis is on gymnastic movement and permanent fixed protection.

Thrutch Awkward, inelegant struggling technique often used in large cracks and chimneys.

Top-rope To climb with the rope belayed or anchored from above.

Top-down Using abseil or a top-rope to pre-inspect, practice or prepare the route before attempting a lead climb.

Traditional climbing, trad An ethic with the emphasis on ground-up, where natural protection and route finding skills are required.

Traverse To climb sideways.

Tufa A fin-like rock formation found in limestone.

Wire, wires A protection nut connected with swaged wire cable.

Zawn Where sea-cliffs form a narrow steep-sided bay.

International Grading Table

AUSTRALIAN	FRENCH	US	UK	UK TECH	
14	4	5.7	HS		4 a
15	5 a	5.8		4 b	
16	5 b		VS		4 c
17	5 c	5.9		5 a	
18	6 a		HVS		
19	6 a +	5.10 a			5 b
20	6 b	5.10 b	E 1	5 c	
21	6 b +	5.10 c	E 2		
		5.10 d			
22	6 c	5.11 a	E 3		6 a
23	6 c +	5.11 b	E 4		
		5.11 c			
24	7 a	5.11 d		6 b	
25	7 a +	5.12 a	E 5		
	7 b	5.12 b			
26	7 b +	5.12 c			
27	7 c	5.12 d	E 6		6 c
28	7 c +	5.13 a			
29	8 a	5.13 b	E 7		
30	8 a +	5.13 c		7 a	
31	8 b	5.13 d	E 8		
32	8 b +	5.14 a			
33	8 c	5.14 b	E 9		
	8 c +	5.14 c			7 b

ACKNOWLEDGEMENTS

Many climbers have been tremendously generous, giving freely of their time and often considerable effort, so as to share their love of climbing. Their enthusiasm is deeply appreciated. Warm and grateful thanks to:

Matt Adams, Chad Albinger, Bryden Allen, Brad Arnold, Jay Audenart, Mark Baker, Rob Baker, Tim Balla, Tony Barten, Anthony Bell, Bobbi Bensman, Simon Birch, Joel Booth, Giles Bradbury, Martin Bride, Donna Bridge, AJ Brown, Gordon Brysland, Steve Bullen, Felicity Butler, Greg Caire, Scott Camps, Kim Carrigan, Greg Child, Gerard Chipper, Garn Cooper, Clive Curson, Paul Cuthbert, Adam Darragh, Paul Deacon, Erik Decamp, Catherine Destivelle, Jocey Dietrich, Adam Donahue, Kate Dooley, Andrew Dunbar, Stefan Eberhard, Sam Edwards, Andrew Ellemor, Rich Emmerson, John Fantini, George Fieg, Silvia Fitzpatrick, Chris Frost, Maureen Gallager, Geoff Gledhill, Jacob Greber, Sarah Green, Emily Grigg, Chad Harder, Brent Hartshorne, Glen Henderson, Tim Hill, Douglas Hockley, Libby Illy, Marcell Jackson, Greg James, Anna Jansen, David Jenkins, Brendan Junge, Venus Kondos, Adrian Laing, Mike Law, Mike Law-Smith, Rob LeBreton, Geoff Little, Chris Loane, Enga Lokey, Stuart Lourding, Gordon Lowe, David Lyons, Boyd MacNamara, Andrew McAuley, Jill McLeod, Robert McMahon, Neil Melion, Garth Miller, Steve Moon, Mike Moore, David Musgrove, Pete Nidd, Megan Osborne, Roger Parkyn, Chris Peisker, Andy Pollitt, Gordon Poultney, Owen Prall, Danelle Rae, Nick Robertson, Richard Rogers, Grant Rowbottom, Chel Roxburgh, Justin Ryan, Louise Shepherd, John Smoothy, Peter Steane, Tara Sutherland, Nick Sutter, Matthew Swaite, Simon Thompson, Lucas Trihey, Hira Verick, Zac Vertrees, Ian Vickers, Nathan Wales, Robert Wall, Chris Warner, Abby Watkins, Amanda Watts, Mike Weeks, Peter Wehr, Roxanne Wells, Huw Widdowson, Jane Wilkinson, Simon Wilson, Kiralee Wood, Vera Wong, Stuart Wyithe, Rod Young, Sue Young and Frey Yule. My apologies to any whose names I have inadvertently neglected.

Very special thanks to those climbers who have consistently been especially helpful and supportive over many years:

Andrew Bull, Robyn Cleland, Kirsty Hamilton, Chris Jones, David Jones, Kieran Lawton, Malcolm Matheson, Simon Mentz, Steve Monks, Greg Moore, and Julian Saunders.

Gratitude to all who specifically contributed to this book:

I have been deeply touched and absolutely delighted with everyone's enthusiasm for the project. My warmest thanks to Anthony Bell, Roger Bourne, AJ Brown, Gordon Brysland, Scott Camps, Greg Child, Robyn Cleland, Mark Colyvan, Adrienne Eberhard, John Ewbank, Chris Frost, Lincoln Hall, Kirsty Hamilton, Peter Jackson, Chris Jones, Mike Law, Kieran Lawton, Rob LeBreton, Kieran Loughran, Gordon Lowe, Robert McMahon, Simon Mentz, Roger Parkyn, Greg Pritchard, Peter Steane, Dave Wagland and Stuart Williams. Thanks also to Greg Pritchard for the introduction and Greg Mortimer for the foreword. And thanks to Bryden Allen, Chris Baxter, Glen Tempest and Lucas Trihey for photographs.

Grateful thanks to all at New Holland who helped turn it all into a reality:

With special praise to my editor Anna Sanders, not least for keeping it all in perspective. And thanks to designer Trinity Loubser-Fry for her vision.

For being especially influential, encouraging, or giving great practical assistance along the way, particular thanks go to:

Chris Baxter, Les Kovacs, Peter Martin, Neil Montgomery, Rudy Panozzo, Lois Perry, Glen Robbins, Samantha Tannous, Glen Tempest and Alan Vogt.

For their assistance thanks also goes to:

Hilary Bennell, Anthony Brennan, Darren Carter, Michelle Doherty, Scott Flower, James Holbrook, Pat and Wynne Jones, Robbie MacKillop, David MacNamara, Doug McLennan, Heather McNair, John Myssonski, Tilly Parkins, Anton Scott-Cameron, Meaghan Vosz and Catherine Woo.

My family has provided invaluable assistance:

Very special gratitude goes to my parents — Keith and Rosemary Carter — who have been a tremendous help, and have also exhibited the most amazing tolerance. And thanks to Jon Richardson, Lyndall Sachs and Andrew Carter who have each generously helped in their own way.

My Nikon gear has performed brilliantly over the years, but in climbing photography you sometimes have to worry more about the rock you are trying to hold onto than what your camera is colliding with. Many thanks to the helpful staff at Maxwell Optics for their assistance when my gear copped too much abuse. Thanks also to Brian Murray's Cameraworld Horsham, Flash Graphics Canberra and Qantas Airlines.

And last but not least, thanks and good karma to the companies that have provided me with quality climbing and outdoor equipment, thereby making my time outdoors and on the cliffs more comfortable, enjoyable, and safer than it would have been: 5.10, Arcteryx, Edelrid, HB, and Mont Adventure Equipment.

Sequence from bottom to top Steve Monks, pitch one (26) Anxiety Neurosis; Felicity Butler pitch two (24) Anxiety Neurosis, *Bluff Major, Mount Arapiles, Victoria.*